A CURIOUS TREE. TRENT AND MERSEY CANAL

Acknowledgements

I would like to thank my mother for initiating the project, my family for their continued support throughout; especially my children Jamie and Eleanor, for their company and encouragement during the preparative stages of the walks. Also the many people who gave freely of their time, knowledge and advice, much of which has been incorporated into the text. Finally I would like to thank David Mitchell and George Power, the publishers for their critical input.

About the author

Chris Buckland has been a teacher for twenty years, for the last ten of which he has taught biology at The King's School, Macclesfield. He lives in Bollington with his wife and two children — a keen walking family. He has enjoyed long-distance walking in Britain, Europe and Africa, and recently covered 3,000 km solo, in the Atlas Mountains, Indonesia, New Zealand and Thailand.

DOG ROSES

CONTENTS

MAP OF THE AREA

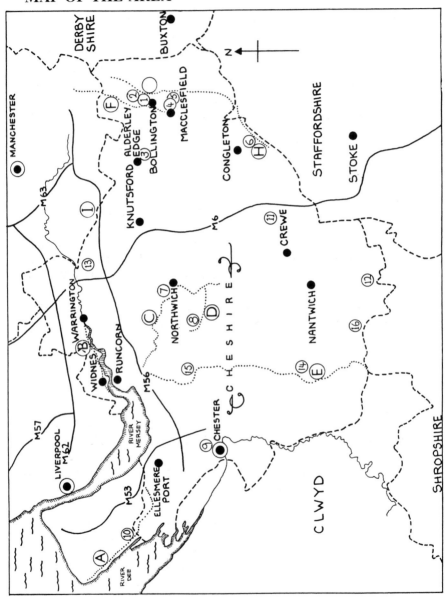

The *numbers* refer to the walks in this book.
The *letters* refer to Long Distance Walks. (See page 75.)

4

Introduction

As a lifelong walker with an insatiable curiosity for the world around me it was a pleasure to be allowed to develop a series of walks in Cheshire. My two children have been my constant companions in this venture and it is my sincere wish that the reader will get as much pleasure from exploring these walks as we had in preparing them. To meet the needs of parents backpacking toddlers, as well as families with teenage children, I have included routes with shorter alternatives and in some cases challenging extensions for the more adventurous and experienced walkers. Being naturally cautious, and the parent of two inquisitive and bouncy children of my own, I have emphasised possible hazards where these exist. Cheshire is a beautiful county with much to lift the human spirit and inspire the imagination. Special features of each walk are highlighted, but the suggestions reflect my own interests and are by no means exhaustive. This is in part deliberate so as not to destroy the sense of wonder that personal exploration and discovery create. It is impossible to explore any one walk fully in a single visit and I hope families will return many times to enjoy a given walk and its surroundings to the full. Some of the walks incorporate sections of Cheshire's famous long distance footpaths. If readers wish to investigate these further a list of these walks is included in the Appendix and their whereabouts is shown on the location map.

Choosing a Walk

Encourage a lifelong interest in walking by selecting a walk or part of a walk that is within the capabilities of the smallest or least experienced member of your party. Allow plenty of time for play and exploration. Children enjoy running ahead to explore, returning to report their findings, before shooting off again. They therefore walk much further than adults. Suitable escape routes are outlined in the text allowing a walk to be cut short. Many of the walks are accessible by car at certain points making rescue of tired or injured walkers possible. The best walks for beginners are those with lots to interest young walkers, with refreshment sites at regular intervals and walks 10 (Parkgate) and 13 (Lymm) fulfil these requirements. Once fitness and confidence have increased more challenging routes such as 5 (Macclesfield Forest), 6 (Mow Cop) and 14 (Raw Head) can be attempted in their entirety. Appendix Two lists the walks in order of their difficulty.

5

Allowing Sufficient Time

These walks are not intended to be route marches and if they are rushed then most of the walks' character will be missed. There is no ideal pace but for planning purposes assume one mile per hour for parties with very young children and two miles per hour for those including eleven year olds. This will vary with weather conditions. Thus allow half to a full day to get the best out of your walk.

What to Wear

English weather is notoriously changeable and it is essential to stay warm and dry for the walk to be enjoyable. This is best achieved by wearing several thin layers of clothing rather than one thick layer, with an outer waterproof cagoule, which also provides a windproof layer. Small children lose body heat faster than their parents and a woolly hat and gloves are invaluable on a cold day. Walking boots are best but in my opinion modern lightweight wellington boots with thick, comfortable socks are a good second and in wet, muddy conditions they have an advantage. In dry conditions well-worn trainers are fine. If my own children are any guide, then whatever the weather they will get wet and muddy and spare clothing is advisable. A small backpack is best for carrying spare clothing, food, cameras, film and first aid which should include plasters, anti-septic wipes and tissues.

The Weather

Walking is a sensual experience which can be extended by walking in different weather conditions. Rain gives any walk new dimensions and the fact that fewer people are about increases the chances of seeing wildlife. It is good sense to check the weather before setting out and to avoid walks 5 and 14 when the weather is poor.

Route Finding

The walks follow public rights of way and concessionary paths. I have included a list of the relevant 1 : 25.000 O.S. maps in the index.

Refreshments

I have included details of a number of public houses and tea rooms at the end of each walk and there are some very attractive picnic sites along each route.

Access by Public Transport   Many of the Walks are accessible by bus or rail. For phone numbers to ring for information see page 76.

Cheshire — A Sketch

Cheshire is an important centre for communication, trade and industry as well as an historically important military site. Wirral, Merseyside and Greater Manchester form the northern border and Cheshire's proximity to Liverpool and Manchester contributed to its commercial growth. The river Mersey and the Manchester Ship Canal encouraged foreign trade. To the east soft red sandstone gives way to harder gritstone with a corresponding hardening of the landscape into the rugged moorlands of the Derbyshire Peak District and the Pennine foothills. South west the moorlands continue into Staffordshire gradually giving way to the softer rural landscape of Shropshire in the south. Wales completes Cheshire's western border.

The Cheshire Plain covers much of the county, with its mixed arable and dairy farming. Black and white Friesian cows enhance the landscape, providing milk for Cheshire Cheese. Speciality red potatoes are sold in market towns such as Knutsford and Sandbach. Rising dramatically from the plain, red sandstone hills traverse the county from north to south. This central Cheshire ridge with its wooded slopes and cliffs, exaggerated by the flatness of the plain, is the unofficial 'Cheshire Way'. Fine views over the surrounding countryside led to its development as a military site and the remains of iron age hill forts and Beeston Castle are evidence of this.

Cheshire has a rich industrial past. Coal and rock salt deposits, together with water power encouraged chemical and textile industries to develop. Natural reserves of rock salt led to the industrialisation of the Weaver valley. Widening and deepening of the river Weaver from Winsford to the Mersey created the 'Weaver Navigation' with its famous Victorian boat lift. Extensive subterranean salt mining resulted in land subsidence and flooding producing the lakes or 'flashes' associated with Winsford. The salt-based industries have declined, although salt is still used to keep British roads ice-free in winter. Oil refineries grew up along the Mersey estuary together with a prosperous petrochemical industry. Textiles also have a long history in Cheshire. Macclesfield and Congleton developed international reputations for silk products while Bollington, Rainow and Styal produced cotton goods. An international airport and Jodrell Bank, with its radio telescope focussed on distant worlds, ensure that Cheshire remains outward looking.

Characteristic architecture includes terraced gritstone cottages of the eastern mill settlements, red sandstone dwellings of the plain and Cheshire brick buildings, typified by the stylish houses of Knutsford and

Wilmslow. The architectural treasury is completed by visually exciting black and white 'magpie' architecture exemplified by the two Moreton Halls, Gawsworth Hall and the houses of Beeston village.

The Romans improved roads, mined, and introduced Christianity to the area. They selected Deva, or Chester as it is now known, as their administrative, legislative and commercial centre. Human activities continued to change the county landscape and not always for the better. However, recent imaginative reclamation of obsolete industrial sites and conservation of natural habitats have provided a wealth of venues for walkers. The unique shallow lakes or meres with their rich and varied wildlife, mosslands, the marshes of the Dee and Mersey estuaries, wild flower meadows, heathery moorlands, deciduous woodland and forest await exploration.

Lewis Carroll, Alan Garner and Elizabeth Gaskell have all found literary inspiration in Cheshire. Thus Alice and the Cheshire Cat, immortalised in stained glass at Daresbury church, and the Wizard of Alderley Edge remain larger than life for many readers, both young and old.

CAVE NEAR STORMY
POINT Route 3

FOXGLOVE

Symbols used on the Route Maps

— ➝ —   Route

- - - - - - -   Footpath not en route

═══════   Road

+++++++++++   Railway

▬▬▬▬▬   Canal

⊃⊂   Bridge

∿∿∿   Stream

➤∿∿➤
F.B.   Footbridge

◢◿◤   Lake

▪▫▪   Building(s)

♧   Quarry

｜｜ ｜｜
ﾉﾉﾉ ﾉﾉﾉ   Marsh

②   Number corresponds with
         route description

10

Middlewood Way and Macclesfield Canal

Outline Bollington ~ Middlewood Way ~ Poynton ~ Canal ~ Bollington.

Summary This is a circular walk along the disused, Macclesfield to Marple railway line to Poynton, returning via the Macclesfield Canal towpath. The old railway has been imaginatively converted into a leisure facility called the Middlewood Way. Both the 'Way' and the towpath are well surfaced and level. Four shorter alternative routes from the Middlewood Way to the canal towpath are also described, following the main route.

Attractions The Viaduct offers excellent views. To the east Clarence Mill, with its prominent red chimney and the Adelphi Mill to the south symbolise Bollington's industrial heritage. To the west the works of Kay Metzeler represent modern industry. Two hills, The Nab and Kerridge hill, surmounted by the famous local monument, White Nancy, complete the distant panorama.

From the viaduct the walk to Poynton enters a cutting, the left hand bank of which has reverted to natural vegetation, unlike the right hand bank which is managed. Badger tracks criss-cross this area. Beside the 'Way' alternative, higher level routes give children the opportunity to explore, yet maintain visual contact with their parents. Between bridges 19 and 20 a dyke, rich in pond life, runs alongside the path. Sticklebacks, newts, frogs and the occasional heron can be seen. In Summer the air is alive with damselflies and dragonflies. Observant walkers may witness the emergence of a dragonfly from its pupa on a reed. After bridge 20 a bridleway runs alongside the footpath. Extensive views of the Cheshire Plain and Woodford Airfield appear on the left. Gliders and other aircraft undergoing tests may be seen overhead. Along the embankment is a seat where walkers can rest awhile, courtesy of Wendy Shanks. The route continues over a small bridge, through a wood and under three more bridges including Street Lane and Schoolfold. The halfway stage is at Wood Lane East bridge. This welcome spot provides the chance to visit one of three refreshment sites or to potter around a small garden centre. Immediately after joining the canal towpath for the return journey there is a pleasant corner to sit and watch the boats, in and around the marina, or to feed the ducks. The towpath provides an easy, scenic route home. The Macclesfield Canal is a relatively new canal,

continued on page 14

11

Route 1

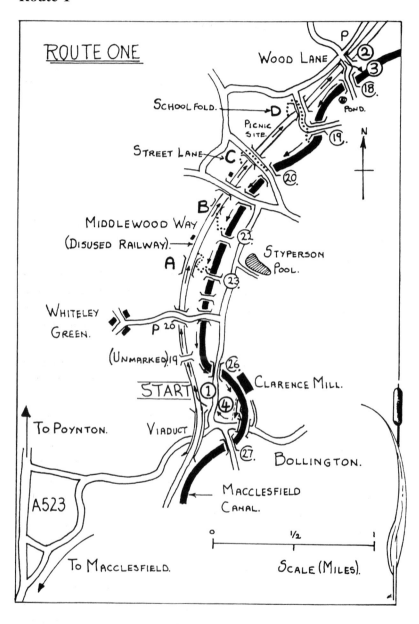

ROUTE ONE

Wood Lane
P
②
③
18.
POND.
SCHOOL FOLD. → D
PICNIC SITE.
19.
N
STREET LANE → C
20.
B
MIDDLEWOOD WAY
(DISUSED RAILWAY). →
21.
STYPERSON POOL.
A
23.
WHITELEY GREEN.
P 20
(UNMARKED) 19
26.
START ①
CLARENCE MILL.
④
TO POYNTON.
VIADUCT
27.
BOLLINGTON.
A523
MACCLESFIELD CANAL.
TO MACCLESFIELD.
0   ½   1
SCALE (MILES).

Route 1

Middlewood Way and Macclesfield Canal 6 miles

START *Adlington road car park Bollington (GR SJ 930779). Take the A523 from Macclesfield and turn right, signposted 'Bollington'. Proceed through the village and under the viaduct, past the Bollington Art Centre and the Methodist Church. Turn left into Adlington road just before the Dog and Partridge. The car park is a hundred yards down on the left. Toilet facilities exist at the start and halfway stage of this walk.*

ROUTE

1. *Climb the setps beside the viaduct, signposted 'Middlewood Way'. With the viaduct behind you follow the linear walkway towards Marple. There is a sign on the end of the viaduct. Proceed to the bridge labelled 'Wood Lane East' which is the sixth bridge crossing over the track.*

2. *Immediately beyond the sixth bridge leave the Middlewood Way by turning left up some steps, signposted '100 m Tea Room/Shop and Miners Arms'. At the top of these steps turn left and cross over the bridge that you have just walked under. Continue in a straight line, keeping Ken's Cabin on the right, to a few steps which lead up on to the canal towpath.*

3. *Turn right under bridge 18 and follow the canal towpath on the right of the canal back to the Clarence Mill in Bollington, which is beyond canal bridge 26. The canal bridges are clearly numbered.*

4. *Opposite the Clarence Mill there is an information board about the mill. Soon after passing this, almost opposite the red chimney, leave the canal by turning right through a gate on your right. Turn left and continue down a rough track to the road. Do not cross the road but turn back on yourself into the receation ground via some green railings. Take a sharp left and go down the steps to the river bridge. Cross over and continue keeping the river on your right. Cross a second bridge and turn left past a weir to the park gate. Cross over the road to the car park opposite.*

SHORTER ALTERNATIVE ROUTES

Transfer from the Middlewood Way to the canal is possible at four points.
A. *(2 MILES)   Passing under the second bridge (labelled '20') the 'Way' passes over a bridge with a farm on the left. Turn right, signposted 'Canal & Sugar Lane', across the field and join the canal at bridge 23.*

featuring attractive gritstone bridges and carved milestones. The milestones, recently restored, were removed, buried or defaced during the last war to confuse or hamper possible enemy invaders. To the left Lyme Park estate can be seen. At bridge 19 wooden 'stop planks' can be seen, which slot into narrow grooves in the canal wall to seal off and drain a section of the canal during maintenance. Wildlife excels and in the early evening bats and water voles go about their business whilst in season Canada geese nest on the far bank. Orchids, marsh marigolds and yellow iris colour the banks, a popular venue for fishermen. At bridge 20 an information board is provided.

Bluebell woodland occurs between bridges 21 and 22. Passing under bridge 25 reveals good views of White Nancy and Bollington. Bridge 26 is skilfully built on an angle and remains a lasting memorial to the stonemason's art. Beyond this bridge Clarence Mill apears. This huge 19th century mill produced high quality cotton goods until the 1960's. The small green bridge over the river in the recreation ground provides the last opportunity to play Pooh sticks today.

Refreshments   (* Denotes easy access from the route)
The Vale, Adlington Road, Bollington. (Beer Garden).*
The Cock and Pheasant, Bollington Road, Bollington. (Beer Garden).
The Church House, Church Street, Bollington. (Children's Room).
The Miner's Arms, Wood Lane, Poynton. (Beer Garden).*
Adlington Village Stores & Tea Room, Wood Lane, Poynton.*
Ken's Cabin, Wood Lane, Poynton.*

———————

B. *(3 MILES) A fourway signpost (Canal/Harrop Green/ Macclesfield/Marple) marks a field track on the right which leads to the canal bridge 22.*

C. *(4 MILES) At Street Lane bridge (signposted) there is a track up to the left which meets a road. Cross the bridge and pass up the very busy road, keeping Springbank Farm on your left, until you find the canal at bridge 20.*

D. *(5 MILES) Before going under Schoolfold bridge take the steps left up to a road. Turn right and walk along the road to join the canal at bridge 19.*

Route 2   6 miles
Bollington to Rainow

Outline   Bollington ~ Ingersley Clough ~ Waulkmill ~ Rainow ~ Bollington.

Summary   A short road walk from Pool Bank car park in Bollington leads to Ingersley Clough, an industrialised valley. The road gives way to a stony track which continues up the valley to Waulkmill. From here a flagged field path leads to the edge of Rainow, a small rural village with an interesting industrial past. Next the route descends to the river Dean before climbing sharply to the side of Kerridge Ridge and the choice of two routes back. The low level route follows an ancient path used by coal miners and quarrymen. The high level route passes along Kerridge Ridge to White Nancy. After a steep descent, a short road walk returns to the car park at Pool Bank.

Attractions   The prosperity of Bollington, an eastern Cheshire cotton mill town, owes much to the industrial revolution of the nineteenth century. Early agricultural settlements scattered along the Dean valley evolved into a thriving industrial town. Raw materials, essential for industrial growth and development, were readily available locally. An abundant supply of soft water, essential in textile processes, also powered the mill machinery. Evidence of water power is found in Ingersley Clough. Thus the weir at Waulkmill, with its impressive waterfall, fed water to the iron aqueduct which passes overhead to the wheelhouse of Ingersley Vale Mill (now Rainow Textiles). The water turned an overshot waterwheel before passing downstream to the mill pool at the start of Ingersley Clough. The canal, which opened in 1831, transported raw materials and finished goods to and from the mills.

     Gritstone, a coarse sandstone quarried locally, was used to build and roof the houses and the steep terraces of stone cottages and flagged streets are an attractive feature of the town. As you cross the flagged field path from Waulkmill to Rainow it is difficult to believe that this was once a busy thoroughfare for cloggen-shod workers passing between the two settlements. It is equally difficult to believe that there were twenty four working mills in Rainow, longsince dismantled to restore its rural status. On the side of Kerridge Ridge black specks of coal can be found and tell tale dips in the hillside mark ancient drift mines. The lower route back follows an ancient track used by coal miners and quarrymen. Active quarrying can be viewed from the ridge, which also provides an aerial

continued on page 18

15

Route 2

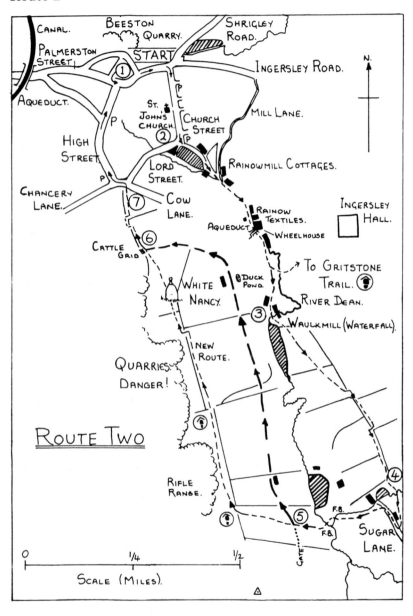

Route 2
Bollington to Rainow
6 miles

START *Pool Bank car park, Bollington (GR SJ 937779). Take the A523 from Macclesfield and turn right at the signpost for Bollington. Continue through the village to the traffic lights. Continue straight on past a row of stone cottages and turn left into the car park at the side of the travel agents.*

ROUTE

1. *Turn left out of Pool Bank car park and walk up Palmerston Street. Cross the main road and take the first right into Church Street. Proceed to the end and turn sharp left at The Crown into Ingersley Vale.*

2. *Follow the road between The Crown public house and Shrigley Dyers past a mill pond on the right and a bowling green on the left. At Rainowmill Cottages the road becomes a stony track. Continue up this track past Rainow Textiles, under an iron aqueduct and on to Waulkmill. At this point an impressive waterfall can be seen.*

3. *At the waterfall there is a gate across the track. Pass through a small gate to the right of the main gate. Bear left up a short rise and pass through a second small gate into a field. Follow the flagstones across two fields and pass through the stone stile in the corner of the second field and turn right. The flagged path now follows the wall/hedge, first on the left and then the right passing through two more stone stiles before reaching a wooden stile at Hough Hole.*

4. *Cross the stile and continue over a brook, up the steps and on to Sugar Lane. Turn right down the lane and turn left at the footpath sign. Carry on straight down the field keeping the stream on your right. Cross two stiles and pass over two footbridges, you are now at the bottom of Kerridge Hill.*

5. *Follow the rough stone steps and then climb diagonally right, up the steep slope ahead to the top of the ridge. Cross over a stile, turn right and follow the Gritstone Way markers (a black footprint on a yellow background) along the ridge to White Nancy. Note the path has been re-routed to avoid the quarry edge. I have labelled this section 'new route' on the map. From White Nancy take the rough path down the hillside until it crosses a well made up track coming from the right. This is the low level alternative route.*

6. *Cross this track and continue down a steep grassy bank. Turn left through a stile, right, and immediately right again via a second stile. Pass down the steps and join Cow Lane at the bottom.*

view of the walk below, including Rainow and Bollington, although Bollington is best seen from the monument White Nancy. This sugar-loaf shaped folly is believed to have been built by the Gaskells to commemorate the Battle of Waterloo and was named after one of the family. It was also an Armada Beacon with a resident lighterman. This walk provides a sharp contrast between the past and present industrial landscape and agriculture scenery.

Refreshments (* Denotes easy access from the walk)
The Church House, Church Street, Bollington. (Children's room)*
The Crown, Church Street, Bollington. (Beer Garden)*

————————

7. *At Cow Lane turn left along Chancery Lane and then right down High Street by the Red Lion. Continue all the way to the bottom. Cross the Road and Pool Bank car park is facing you.*

LOW LEVEL ALTERNATIVE ROUTE: Follow the steps in '5' but only climb one third of the way up the hillside to meet a well trod, grassy track coming from the gate on your left. Turn right and follow this track. It will pass two houses, the second with a small duck pond. Shortly after this the track joins a road. Turn left and follow the track round below White Nancy until it comes to the second cattle grid. Do not cross the second grid but turn right down the steep grassy bank and then continue as for '6' above.

NEAR ALDERLEY EDGE

18

Alderley Edge

Outline Information Centre ~ Goldenstone ~ Hough Level ~ Saddlebole ~ Stormy Point ~ Armada Beacon ~ Information Centre.

Summary The main walk is relatively short and on well surfaced tracks which are steep in parts, although the steep sections can be avoided by turning left at Golden Stone and going direct to Stormy Point. The walk provides exciting opportunities for children of all ages to explore and extra miles can be added on in seeking out the popular landmarks. Thus a main route is described, with the tracks leading to specific sites of interest included as detours.

Note The defined footpaths are safe but once off these paths, steep slopes, exposed cliffs and rough stones are potentially dangerous.

Attractions Alderley Edge is a richly wooded, red sandstone escarpment famous for mining, folklore and spectacular views. There is a National Trust information centre at the start of the walk.

Bronze Age man was attracted to the blue and green tinged sandstone of Alderley Edge, fragmenting the rock with fire and primitive tools, remains of which have been discovered by archaeologists. Wood from the area was burnt in order to extract copper, which alloyed with tin made bronze. Advances in mining technology created extensive underground passages some of which can be visited by prior arrangement with Derbyshire Caving Club (Tel: Chapel-en-le-Frith — 3151). Engine Vein Mine and Stormy Point are open-cast mines and well worth careful exploration (a torch would be useful). Saddlebole was an ancient hearth for the smelting of ore. Blue flecks of malachite and azurite can still be seen in the sandy soil. Hough level is currently being excavated and the railway is used for bringing out silt.

The 'Edge' is steeped in legend and many songs and tales of magic have originated here. Alan Garner's story, The Weirdstone Of Brisingamen, keeps this magic alive and many local features are referred to in his book. The Wizard's Well and Holy Well provide water with mystical properties from springs which run into stone troughs. The Wizard's Well has the legend 'Drink of this and drink thy fill for the water falls by the wizard's will' and a face carved into the rock above it. A reminder that beneath the Edge one hundred knights and their snow white chargers lay sleeping, watched over by Merlin, awaiting the day

continued on page 22

Route 3

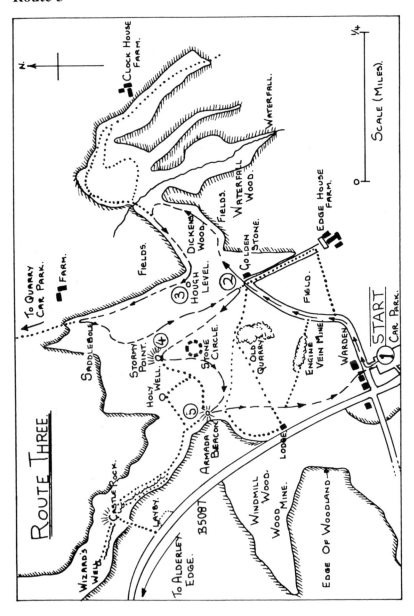

Route 3
Alderley Edge
3 miles

START   *The National Trust car park at Alderley Edge (GR SJ 860773). The car park can be found one mile from Alderley Edge on the B5087, Macclesfield to Alderley Edge road. It is clearly signed just before the Wizard Inn restaurant.*

ROUTE

1. *From the car park head towards the white information building. Turn right up the private road past the warden's house and continue to Golden Stone, where the road turns sharp right.*

2. *Ignore the wooden barrier on the left and proceed straight ahead on to a well defined path. Follow this downhill and around a left-hand hairpin bend to a field at the bottom. Turn left and follow the field edge bearing right to Hough Level.*

3. *Continue along the edge of the field until you come to a barrier. Pass under the barrier and turn sharp left up a rough bridleway. After crossing a rough stony area continue to a second stony area. Bear slightly left and drop down a little until a large mouthed cave can be seen to your right. Walk past the cave mouth and up a steep narrow track bearing right. At the top of the steps turn left and follow the path until it meets a well defined wheelchair path. Turn right and proceed straight to Stormy Point.*

4. *Turn left almost back on yourself. This wide level track passes the Druid's circle on the left before arriving at the Armada Beacon, a small stone monument.*

5. *Stand such that you can read the legend on the Beacon Monument. The stepped path down to the left leads to Holy Well, Castle Rock and Wizard's Well. At the bottom of the steps turn left and soon a few steps to the right mark a steep descent to the Holy Well. Retrace your steps from Holy Well, turning right on regaining the main path. Continue until the path divides into two. The higher of the two paths passes along the top of a sandstone edge while the lower one runs along the bottom of the same edge and is the safer of the two. Both lead to Castle Rock. Continue past Castle Rock along the lower path until you come to the Wizard's Well.*

6. *Retrace your steps to Armada Beacon. Face the Beacon once again but this time turn right down to a horizontal tree. Take the Wheelchair path to the left of this tree. Follow this path straight ahead, over the crossroads, past Engine Vein on the left and drop down to the car park in front of you.*

when England shall have need of them. The Devil's Grave at Stormy Point is best viewed from below. The Druidic stone circle between the point and the Beacon is a folly.

The finest views are obtained from Stormy Point, Castle Rock and to a lesser extent Armada Beacon now surrounded by trees. The Beacon was the site of a tower destroyed by gales in 1931. The views from Stormy Point are especially attractive because they are framed by Scots pine, introduced to reafforest the Edge after the trees had been removed for smelting ore. This is a charming walk with a mystical quality about it.

Refreshments National Trust Tea Room. Alderley Edge. Not always open.

Vans selling a variety of goods operate in the car park especially during weekends.

A variety of refreshment places can be found in Alderley Edge itself.

DEVA TERRACE AND RIVER BOAT Route 9

Route 4   3 miles
Tegg's Nose

Outline   Windyway car park ~ Tegg's Nose ~ Bottoms Reservoir ~ Windyway car park.

Summary   The walk is divided into two, a high level circuit around Tegg's Nose summit and a more demanding lower level route along the lower slopes. The fact that the site is a disused quarry means that the terrain is stony and rough. Exposed cliff edges, especially around the hole, are potentially very dangerous and children should not be left unsupervised.

Attractions   Tegg's Nose is the largest of several millstone grit quarries cut into the ridge and was the source of good quality building stone until 1955. In 1972 the area was designated a country park which is divided into two separate parts, Windy Way and Tegg's Nose. Windy Way, which is accurately named, provides good facilities including toilets, an information centre and an excellent picnic site. Tegga, the giant guardian of this site, can be found sleeping in a secluded corner but if you find him do not disturb his rest. A view point gives excellent views of the hill farms below, their chequered fields edged by dry stone walls a product of these quarries. Within the fields Derbyshire Gritstone sheep can be seen which are very resistant to the cold, wet conditions found here, especially during the lambing season. This view is set against the backdrop of Macclesfield Forest with Shuttlingsloe rising majestically above it.

The second site is reached via a concessionary footpath and it was here that Granada Television filmed the children's film 'Ghost Story' during the Spring of 1989. An open air quarry museum gives an insight into the work that once went on here. The large hole near the exhibition centre provided high quality stone for decorative stonework. More recently its steep sides have been used for supervised abseilling. Two further viewpoints, each with photographic explanations of the scenery, can be found on this site. The lower viewpoint overlooks the reservoirs, a centre for bird-watching and private fishing, and Langley, once famous for button making, silk processing and the artist Charles Tunnicliffe. The highest view point looks to the horizon in every direction. The beautifully restored Saddler's Way, part of an ancient packhorse trail, is a fitting end to a lovely walk.

The park provides an excellent programme of events, details of which can be obtained from the information centre, as well as an orienteering course.

continued on page 26

23

Route 4

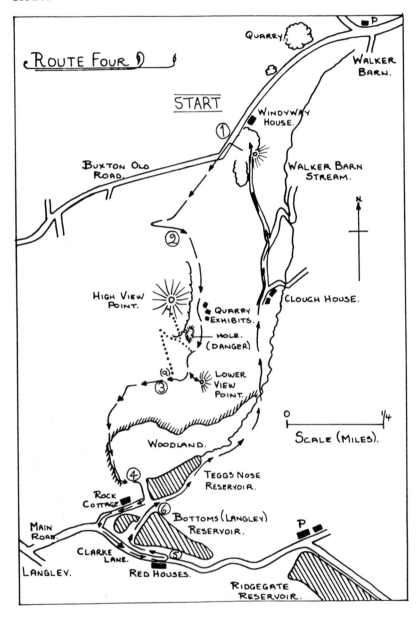

Route 4

Tegg's Nose   3 miles

START *Windy Way car park (GR 951732), two miles east of Macclesfield. Take the A537 towards Buxton and turn right into Buxton Old Road which is signed 'Country Park'. Continue up this road and the car park is signposted right 'Country Park' at Windy Way Head.*

ROUTE

1. *Walk out of the car park entrance keeping the information centre on your right. Turn left signposted 'Croker Hill'. The walk follows the Gritstone Trail which is waymarked with a footprint on a yellow circle. It also follows a local walk waymarked with red dots. Follow either of these waymarks and pass through two stiles until you reach a 'Country Park' boundary stone.*

2. *Continue straight ahead and bear left at a second stone signposted 'Tegg's Nose Summit'. Several other unmarked paths exist which should be ignored. A quarry exhibition appears on the left and a cliff of broken rock on the right, where a danger of falling rock exists. Next the path skirts around a very deep hole on the right. Walk along one side of this and then proceed straight ahead along a small path signed with a Gritstone Trail logo. A small track leads off to the left immediately before a pronounced bump and opposite an orienteering point 'M+'. This short detour leads to the lower viewpoint above the reservoirs. After admiring the view retrace your steps back to the main path which circles around until a stile is reached on the left. The stile is opposite a picnic table and labelled with a small plaque 'Langley' and a Gritstone Trail waymark.*

2(a). *If you wish to see the second viewpoint do not cross the stile but carry on past the stone marked 'Car Park' following the blue markers. Turn right and then left, before the hole, up a wide track leading to the high viewpoint, which is clearly visible against the skyline.*

   NOTE   *This viewpoint is very exposed and best avoided with small children and in windy weather. Retrace the path back to the stile in 2.*

   NOTE   *It is possible to avoid the strenuous lower route at this stage by following the blue circles back in the direction signed 'Car Park'.*

3. *Cross over the stile and follow the red waymarks down to the edge of the country park, located at the bottom of a flight of steps.*

4. *Turn right and walk over the dam and then right again into*

Refreshments   During the Summer refreshments are available from the Centre at Tegg's Nose. In addition ice cream vans are available at weekends.

The Leathers Smithy Inn — Opposite Ridgegate reservoir — Beer Garden.

The Setter Dog Inn, Walker Barn, Buxton Road.

Holehouse Lane, signposted 'Langley'. Pass Rock Cottage and continue along the lane until it joins 'Main Road'. Turn left and walk up Clarke Lane along the edge of Bottoms Reservoir as far as Red Houses.

5.   *Turn left through the gap in the wall, signposted 'Tegg's Nose'. Back track along the side of the reservoir before turning right over the dam. The gate at the end of the dam ends this circular detour.*

6.   *Turn right at the gate and follow the 'Bridlepath' sign. From here the way is well marked with red circles back up to the car park. Walk up the lane and turn left at a stone marked 'Forest Chapel/Car Park', across the stepping stones to a stile. Cross the stile, turn right and continue to a gate/stile. Follow the stone sign 'Car Park'. Soon the path joins a road beside Clough House. Bear left and after a short while turn left, signed 'Car Park', up the beautifully restored Saddlers Way. This returns to the third viewpoint and the starting point.*

LARCH

26

Route 5   5–6 miles
Macclesfield Forest

Outline   Trentabank ~ Ridgegate Reservoir ~ Macclesfield Forest ~ Toot Hill ~ Trentabank.

Summary   This is the Cheshire Peak District at its best with spectacular views and rugged remote countryside. It is the most challenging walk in this series involving steep ascents and descents over rough often very muddy ground. A great deal of imaginative work is being done to improve existing paths and create new ones. The complete walk should not be undertaken lightly. It has been divided into three circular sections. Circuit one is less demanding but gives a taste of the area. The second circuit is physically very demanding whilst the third circuit is a comfortable walk and could be attempted in isolation, starting at the car park.

Attractions   Macclesfield Forest is an area of afforestation covering the lower slopes of Shuttlingsloe, a prominent conical landmark, in eastern Cheshire. The trees are mainly coniferous including Larch, Sitka Spruce and Pine. Thousands of Norway Spruce find their way into people's homes each year to become Christmas Trees. Beech and Sycamore can also be found. This forest, together with Mara or Delamere Forest as it is now known is one of two surviving ancient forests in Cheshire. The other two, Wirral and Mondriem, have disappeared. The occasional red deer can be seen, possibly descended from ancestral stock hunted by royalty when the forest was a royal hunting forest. High rainfall makes it an ideal water catchment area for four reservoirs, two of which feature in the walk. The rainfall also means it is often very muddy in parts. The area is a fully functional working environment and both forestry and water board workers can be seen going about their business.

During the Spring Trentabank reservoir is the scene of much excitement for it is here that many herons return to mate and reclaim their tree top nests. The heronry attracts many bird-watchers to the area but the majestic flight of these huge birds and their courtship activities cannot fail to impress even the non-enthusiast. The reservoir is also a nature reserve for other wildlife.

In the hamlet of Macclesfield Forest a small church can be found dedicated to St. Stephen, a Christian who was stoned to death for his beliefs. The Forest Chapel as it is better known has been the site of worship for over three hundred years. Its simplicity and isolation provide

continued on page 30

27

Route 5

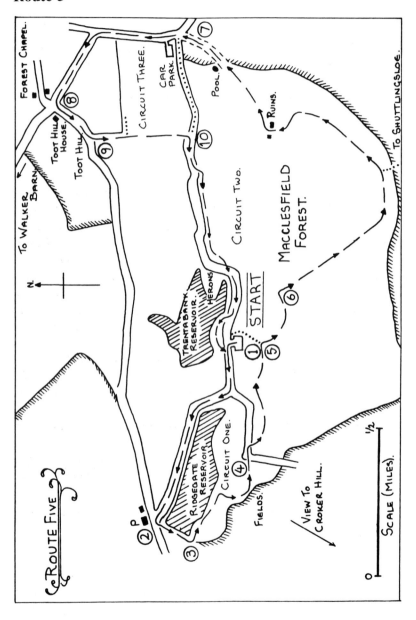

Route 5

Macclesfield Forest   5–6 miles

START   *Take the A523 from Macclesfield to Leek and turn left into Byrons Lane signposted 'Sutton/Langley/Wincle'. Turn left signposted 'Langley' and continue through Langley village. Bear right at the Leathers Smithy public house and continue past Ridgegate reservoir. The car park is up this road, on the right, opposite Trentabank reservoir. (GR 962712)*

ROUTE

1. *Turn left out of the car park and walk back down the road, past Ridgegate reservoir to the Leathers Smithy public house.*

2. *Opposite the Leathers Smithy a path signposted 'footpath' and waymarked with a '3' leads across the dam. Turn left along this path.*

3. *At the end of the dam there is a gate and a stile signposted 'Shuttlingsloe via forest trail'. Turn left through the stile and follow the yellow arrows marked with a '3' until you come to a road.*

4. *Proceed straight down the road for a short distance before turning right on to a waymarked footpath which runs parallel to the road initially. Follow the sign to 'Shuttlingsloe' and continue in a straight line (do not turn right) following the waymarks until you come to a three way signpost.*

   NOTE   *At this stage it is possible to return to the car park by following the sign to Trentabank having completed a circular walk (circuit one). The next stage is demanding both in terms of distance and terrain.*

5. *Turn right signposted 'Shuttlingsloe' up a stony track until you reach a second three way signpost.*

6. *Once again turn right into the forest to begin a long steep muddy climb. After half a mile a footpath leads off right to Shuttlingsloe. Ignore this and follow the waymarks for another half a mile along a well surfaced stony track until you reach a gate/stile leading on to a road.*

   NOTE   *It is possible to turn left down the road at this stage thus completing circuit two.*

7. *Cross over the stile and walk straight ahead past a car park on your left. Do not follow the waymarks into the car park but stay on the road until you come to a sign 'Forest Chapel' pointing left. Turn left up this road to the Forest Chapel crossroads.*

29

a refuge from the humdrum of daily life and an opportunity for spiritual recovery. On the first Sunday after August the twelfth an annual rush-bearing ceremony takes place in the chapel and many pilgrims walk to the chapel for this occasion.

This walk has a lot to offer but is best done in good weather.

Refreshments The Leathers Smithy Inn, Clarke Lane, Langley. (Beer Garden)

---

8. *Turn left at Toot Hill House signposted 'Langley 2½'. Walk down the road for a little way before turning left over a stile, just before a wood.*

9. *Follow the path down between the field and the wood and continue in a straight line until you meet a road.*

10. *Turn right down the road until you come to Trentabank reservoir. NOTE If you prefer you can turn left on to a new footpath which runs parallel to the road. This is preferable to walking down the road and the path rejoins the road lower down. At Trentabank a short circular detour is reached through a small gate to the right of the road giving good views of the reservoir and heronry.*

MARBURY ACROSS BIG MERE Route 16

6 miles

Mow Cop

Outline Mow Cop Castle ~ The Old Man Of Mow Cop ~ Ackers Crossing ~ Kent Green ~ Mount Pleasant ~ Mow Cop.

Summary From the famous monument Mow Cop Castle the walk continues on high ground to the Old Man of Mow Cop. It then descends gently through mixed deciduous woodland and farmland to the canal towpath which is comfortable walking. It then climbs steadily up through woodland and fields to Mount Pleasant. The last section includes a sharp ascent through a series of abandoned quarries and the village of Mow Cop.

Attractions Mow Cop is derived from 'Moel Cop' meaning bald rock or exposed summit and upon its summit a ruined castle stands. Mow Cop Castle dominates the skyline and was built in 1754 by Squire Randle Wilbraham to enhance the view from his living-room at Rhode Hall. Although built as a folly it was used as a Summer House. The site had previously been used as an Armada Beacon which is not surprising as the extensive views overlook seven counties. Three long distance walks converge on the castle, the Staffordshire Way, the Mow Cop Trail and the South Cheshire Way.

The rock is a powerful symbol for Methodists for it was here in 1807 that the Primitive Methodists or Ranters as they were better known broke from the Wesleyan tradition. A stone commemorating this event can be seen on the way up to the castle. One hundred years later a hundred thousand pilgrims visited the site. Evidence of these events is apparent in local street names and from the numerous Methodist chapels found in the area.

Quarrying was the main occupation and circular marks on the rock faces mark where millstones were cut out and a part completed stone can be found below the castle on its eastern side. Quarrying created the Old Man Of Mow Cop, a seventy foot high pinnacle of rock now sadly degenerating and recent falls of rock are visible. Just above the Old Man a stone marked with the letters S and C marks the boundary between Staffordshire and Cheshire.

The canal passes the lovely Ramsdell Hall and provides an opportunity to make a detour to Little Moreton Hall.

Refreshments (* Easily Accessible)
The Globe Inn (Drumber Lane, Mow Cop).

continued on page 34

31

Route 6

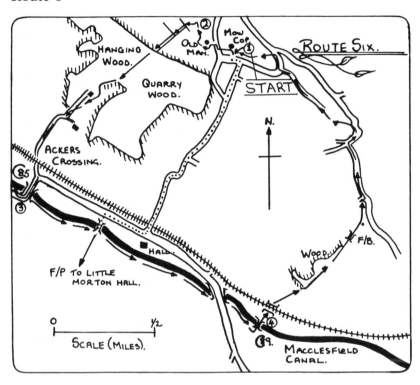

GORSE   gold   all months

Route 6

Mow Cop   6 miles

START   *The National Trust car park at Mow Cop Castle (GR 857573).*
Take the A34 from Congleton towards Newcastle and turn left at
Astbury signposted 'Great Moreton Hall and Mow Cop'. Continue
past the entrance to Great Moreton Hall and over a canal bridge.
Continue along the road to a sign 'stop when lights show'. Shortly after
this sign turn left into Drumber Lane. Cross the level crossing and
continue straight to the top. Turn left and then right into the car park
below Mow Cop Castle.

ROUTE

1. *From the car park take the stony, stepped track to the left of the*
   information board towards the folly. Halfway up, a stone
   commemorating the Primitive Methodists can be seen. Turn left at this
   stone and follow the yellow South Cheshire Way marks (an arrow and
   the letters SCW) towards The Old Man Of Mow Cop, which is just
   visible behind the houses to the north. At the road turn right and then
   left on to a path signposted 'Ackers Crossing'. Continue past The Old
   Man and head for the radar tower ahead.

2. *Shortly before the tower turn left down a track signed 'Footpath'. The*
   section of the walk to the railway crossing is waymarked although the
   yellow SCW marks are not always obvious. The way leads down to a
   stile and across two fields to a wood through which a well trod path
   leads to a stile. Turn right down the field path, past a farm to a small
   gate. Pass through the gate and turn left down the sandy lane until you
   reach a railway crossing. Continue down the road to the T junction.
   Cross the road with care and turn right, past a telephone box and over
   canal bridge 85.

3. *Immediately turn sharp right and descend the steps beside the bridge to*
   the canal towpath. Walk under bridge 85 and along the towpath,
   passing under three unmarked bridges, to bridge 89. Just before bridge
   89 leave the towpath by turning right and then left in order to cross over
   canal bridge 89.

4. *Cross over the stile beyond the canal bridge and proceed straight up the*
   field path and under the railway. Continue through the wood keeping
   the stream on your left, to a field. Bear slightly left to a gap in the hedge
   and cross over a footbridge. Continue straight ahead to an isolated stile
   in the middle of the field. From here head towards the lone telegraph
   pole and bear left towards the corner of the field, where a stile leads on

The Cheshire View (Mow Cop).
The Rising Sun (Kent Green).*
The Bird In Hand (Kent Green).*
The Three Horseshoes (Kent Green).
The Post Office/Shop (Mount Pleasant).*

———————

to a road. Turn left and walk up the road to the junction. Turn right along Chapel Street. The road bears left and at this point take the footpath to the left signposted 'Mow Cop'. This steep, scruffy track passes steeply up through quarries and widens out into a rough track. Follow it upwards until the Castle suddenly comes into view. At the road turn right and just past Hillside Methodist Chapel turn left up a track between the houses, across a road, up a few steps and Mow Cop Castle is ahead of you. If you do not wish to climb over the rock to the car park proceed to the left.

MARSH MARIGOLDS

Marbury Country Park and Anderton

Outline   Marbury Country Park ~ Budworth Mere ~ Anderton ~ Marbury Country Park.

Summary   This is a level plains walk and the going is easy. The walk starts in Marbury Country Park and proceeds along well-managed paths. It continues along a well-surfaced towpath and finally across fields to the park. There are some muddy sections through the woods but these are minimal. There are numerous stiles to climb over in the last section of the walk.

Attractions   A walk in 'Beauty and the Beast' tradition, with the beauty of Marbury Park sharply contrasted to the ugliness of the industrial landscape of Northwich, the capital of Vale Royal. Marbury's history is mostly speculative, being based upon stories and folklore rather than fact.

The house, modelled on the palace of Fontainbleau, together with much of its recorded history have disappeared. The landscaped gardens remain, visually enriched by the wide variety of trees. Similarly Bigwood, a mature deciduous woodland, is made more interesting by the inclusion of exotic tree species.

In the car park Elmer, a powerful Constantine Smith sculpture carved from a tree, symbolises hope for the future of Marbury's trees. Budworth Mere, once an ancient fish hatchery and more recently a bird sanctuary, is famous for grebe, which can be viewed from the hide overlooking the reedbeds. Its beautiful setting, with the village of Great Budworth in the distance, makes a walk along its shore a therapeutic experience. Look out for the remains of the ice house, a device designed to store winter ice during the Summer months, used to chill food and wine. A cock fighting pit is a reminder of the barbarous pastimes enjoyed by our ancestors. The slipway originally provided a link to Great Budworth. The mere and woods are a haven for wildlife so look out for foxes, owls and the yellow flash of flags and marsh marigold in the wetter areas. Rock salt was mined at Marbury for use in the local chemical industry. Although the Trent and Mersey canal carried salt it was built by Josiah Wedgwood to carry raw materials, including china clay from Liverpool to the Potteries and finished products in the reverse direction. The Anderton boat lift provided an important link to the Weaver Navigation. Looking down from the canal, over Winnington, one can

continued on page 38

Route 7

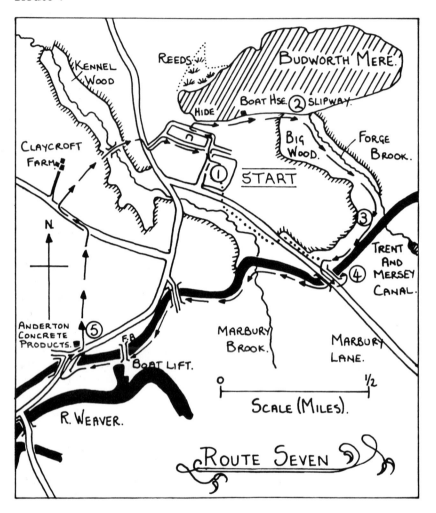

REEDS

KENNEL WOOD

BUDWORTH MERE.

BOAT HSE ② SLIPWAY.

HIDE

CLAYCROFT FARM

BIG WOOD.

FORGE BROOK.

① START

N

③

TRENT AND MERSEY CANAL.

④

ANDERTON CONCRETE PRODUCTS.

⑤

F.B

BOAT LIFT.

MARBURY BROOK.

MARBURY LANE.

0   ½

SCALE (MILES).

R. WEAVER.

ROUTE SEVEN

Route 7

Marbury Country Park and Anderton $3\frac{1}{2}$ miles

START *Marbury Country Park car park (GR 652763). Proceed along Watling Street through Northwich. Cross over the swing bridge and turn right signposted 'Victoria Infirmary and Winnington'. At the end of Winnington Lane cross a second swing bridge and turn right signed 'Anderton and Marbury Country Park'. The country park is signposted right after passing through Anderton. Toilets are provided near the information centre.*

ROUTE

1. *Leave the car park via the entrance. Turn right, through a gate and follow the road to a junction. Bear left and follow this road past the information centre signposted 'Mere/Bird Hide'. The road veers left before it straightens out. Halfway along this section turn right down a series of steps, which lead to a bird hide on the mere side. Turn right and continue along the side of the mere until you reach the slipway.*

2. *At the slipway turn right and leave the mere side. A short ascent leads to a wide track. Turn left signposted 'Canal via Big Wood'. Follow this track through the woods bearing left at the fork and continue to the canal.*

3. *The woodland path follows the canal before veering right. Shortly after this a stake with the number 15 on it will be seen to the right of the path. (NOTE At this point you can shorten the walk by staying on the wide path and following it back to the car park.) Opposite marker 15 turn left along a narrow path which leads to a road. Turn left and walk up the road, over the canal bridge and left down the steps on to the canal towpath.*

4. *Turn left under the bridge and continue along the towpath with the canal on your right. Pass the Anderton boat lift to the left and continue to the next road bridge over the canal. Immediately before this bridge turn left up the track to the road. Turn right over the canal and continue up the road for a short way. Cross the road and turn left along the footpath beside Anderton Concrete Products.*

5. *The last stage follows field paths and crosses ten stiles before regaining the car park. Follow the footpath to a stile and bear right to a second stile. Continue in the same direction, towards a house, over three more stiles to a road. Turn left and walk along the road until a stile can be seen in the hedge to the right. Cross this stile and walk straight down two fields, through a small wood and over a further field to a road.*

appreciate the contribution made by the salt-based chemical industry, especially the soda ash works initiated by Brunner and Mond, to the prosperity of Northwich. Many local buildings and the canal at Marbury have subsided as a result of underground salt mining. Less obvious, but at one time almost as important as the salt workings, was the shipbuilding that once went on here and it is hard to believe that eight hundred ships were built in fifty years by W. J. Yarwoods. They, together with their rivals Isaac Pimblott and Sons, made a major contribution to the war efforts of the two great wars.

Refreshments   The park is an ideal place for a picnic and facilities are provided. Ice cream vendors operate in the car park and two venues on the canal cater for families. A restaurant at the Anderton Marina beside IML cruisers can be reached by crossing canal bridge 198. The Stanley Arms is reached via the footbridge opposite the Anderton boat lift.

Cross over the road and turn right. After a short distance turn left signposted 'Marbury Hall Nurseries'. Continue straight ahead and just past the gate turn right. This leads past the site of Marbury House and on to a sandy path which leads past the toilets and back to the car park.

HAWTHORN

38

Whitegate Way and Newchurch Common

Outline   Whitegate Station ~ Kennel Lane ~ Newchurch Common ~ Common Lane ~ Marton Hole ~ Whitegate Station.

Summary   The outward journey follows part of the Whitegate Way, a pleasant level walk along a disused railway line to Kennel Lane. This section offers alternative pathways alongside the main track, which children can explore safely. The return path follows sandy tracks and farm roads back to Whitegate Station from where a short loop walk via Marton Hole can be used to extend this delightful walk.

Attractions   During the 1880's a short railway line carried salt from the mines at Winsford to Cuddington. The disused line has been replaced by a very pleasant linear walkway which is shared by walkers and horseriders. The tree lined track is a pleasant walk on a hot day. The excavation of sand from this area has left several large shallow lagoons. Some are overgrown and provide excellent habitats for wildlife. One has been developed by a local water ski club for recreational use. It is exciting to watch the more advanced jumping from the specially built ramp. Although used mainly by water skiers, wind surfers and sub aqua divers may also be seen enjoying the facilities. It is an historically interesting area for it was here that the Cistercian monks built their largest abbey, together with supporting farms and fish ponds. Surprisingly little evidence of the monk's presence remains, except in a few local place names, for example, Abbotsmoss plantation. This has recently been felled and replanted. Nearby Kennel Lane takes its name from the Cheshire Kennels, home to the Cheshire Hounds, which can sometimes be seen exercising in the locality. The section of the Whitegate Way used to extend the walk is rich in wild flowers. It passes through pleasant farmland in which is found a large, steep sided pond, known as Marton Hole. Driving back towards Whitegate village, a fine collection of Beech trees towers over the junction of Daleford Lane and Clay Lane. Whitegate village with its delightful thatched cottages, St. Mary's church and village green is well worth visiting.

Refreshments   There are excellent toilet and picnic facilities at Whitegate Station but there are no refreshments available here or on the walk itself. However, there is a public house in Whitegate called the Plough, which has a beer garden. To find this you must return to

continued on page 42

Route 8

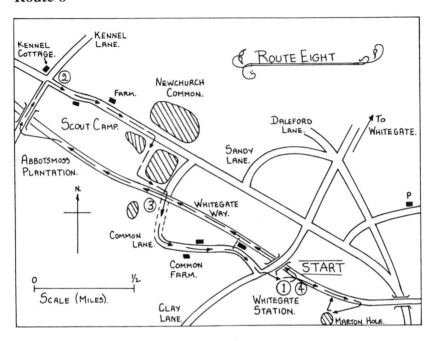

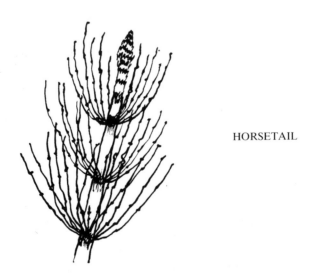

HORSETAIL

Route 8

Whitegate Way and Newchurch Common 5 miles

START *Whitegate Station (GR 624676). Take the A556 from Manchester towards Chester until you reach the traffic lights at Sandiway. Turn left into Dalefords Lane and continue along this road to a sign 'Whitegate Way'. Turn right into Clay Lane and continue, over a railway bridge, before turning sharp left into the car park at Whitegate Way Station. There is an information board, toilets and a very pleasant picnic area on this site.*

ROUTE

1. *From the information board cross on to the bridleway/footpath. Turn left, go under a bridge and follow the Whitegate Way towards Sandiway, until you see a second bridge over the 'Way'. Leave Whitegate Way by turning left just before this bridge, up a short track. At the top turn right, over the bridge and follow the sandy track, called Kennel Lane, to a crossroads.*

2. *Turn right at the crossroads along the lane beside the Cheshire County Scout Council Forest Camp. Continue, past a large open expanse of water on your left. A second expanse of water, the home of Sandiway Water Ski Club, appears on your right. Immediately before this lake, turn right over a stile and follow the path, keeping the lake on your left, to a second stile. At this stile turn right, through the gate and continue straight over the Whitegate Way in the direction of 'Clay Lane', which is signposted.*

3. *A wide grassy track leads over a field and then bears left past Common Farm. Continue along Common Lane to the 'T' junction at Clay Lane. Turn left up the road and then right to Whitegate Station signposted 'Whitegate Way Car Park'.*

3(a). *Common Lane passes very close to the Whitegate Way at Vale Royal Stables making a shortcut possible. Take the footpath to the left, beside the stables, and turn right along the 'Way' back to Whitegate Station.*

4. *To extend this walk continue, past the toilets and straight down the Whitegate Way until you see a gate across the track. Shortly before this a footpath leads off to the right signposted 'Marton Hole and Chester Lane'. Follow this footpath diagonally across the field to a stile on the other side. Cross over and walk to the edge of Marton Hole, a large pond. Turn around and a second stile can be seen.*

Daleford Lane. Turn right at the Beeches and then take the first left into Beauty Bank. There are also refreshments available at Knight's Grange which is one and a half miles south east of Whitegate village along Grange Lane.

Cross over this stile and a field path leads straight back on to the Whitegate Way. Turn left and return to the car park.

THE OLD DEE BRIDGE

Chester — Historic Walls and Water Meadows

Outline   The Old Dee Bridge, Chester ~ The Meadows ~ Dukes Drive ~ Chester City Walls ~ The Old Dee Bridge.

Summary   This walk combines the historic walls of Chester with a level riverside walk through The Meadows and a pleasant return to the city via Dukes Drive through the Eaton Estate. Although easy walking the Meadows will be muddy after rain. The Meadows offer no chance of buying refreshment en route but excellent opportunities for a picnic. The walls on the other hand can be left at various points and refreshment is never far away in the city.

Attractions   Chester's two thousand years of architectural heritage began with the Roman fort of Deva, built on the border to resist Welsh invasion. Looking across to the Welsh hills the strategic importance of Chester is apparent. Welsh invaders still cross the Old Dee Bridge, but they come in friendship, to enjoy the charming city, as tourists. The design and fortifications of the city owe much to the Roman influence but civil war, religion, plague and modern planners have helped to restructure it. Built on the edge of the river Dee meant that Chester was a once a great port, trading principally with Ireland and Europe. Originally the river flowed past the Watergate and clustered around the walls were the storehouses and paraphernalia associated with shipping. It ceased to be a port when the river silted up, redirecting the river and creating new land known as the Roodee. This has always been an important sporting venue and football was banned here during the sixteenth century because of hooliganism, a prophetic move! It is the home of Chester races, a course with a long and fine tradition. The great cathedral stands on a site used for worship for a thousand years and names like Black Friars, Grey Friars, White Friars and Nuns Road confirm that religion played an important role in the city's development. The Rows are unique and a romantic place to walk and shop. Another famous building bears the legend 'God's Providence is mine' as a memorial to the fact that it was not infected by the plague. The attractive Bridge of Sighs and the Bluecoats School have a sinister side, for it was across this bridge that condemned prisoners went to hear the last rites in the school chapel. The local town crier operates from the needle-like monument, called the Cross, in the town centre. With so much history it is no surprise to find that Chester has many fine museums including the Heritage Centre and

continued on page 46

Route 9

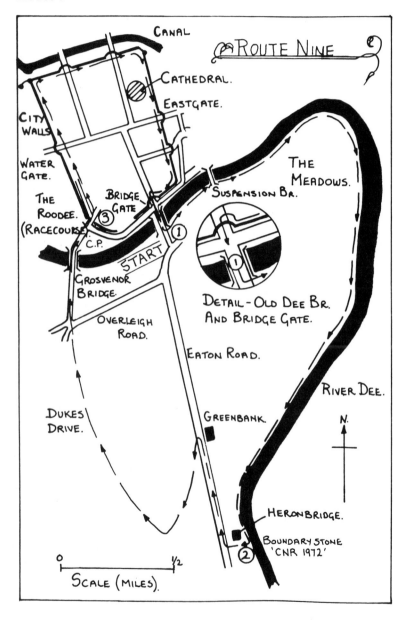

Canal

Route Nine

Cathedral.

Eastgate.

City Walls

Water Gate.

The Roodee. (Racecourse)

Bridge Gate

③

C.P.

The Meadows.

Suspension Br.

Start

①

Detail - Old Dee Br. And Bridge Gate.

Grosvenor Bridge.

Overleigh Road.

Eaton Road.

River Dee.

N.

Dukes Drive.

Greenbank

Heronbridge.

Boundary Stone 'CNR 1972'

②

0 ½

Scale (miles).

Route 9

Chester — Historic Walls and Water Meadows 6 miles

START *The Old Dee Bridge in Chester (GR 407658). Take the A51 to Chester and follow the signs 'City Centre'. Enter the city walls via Newgate. Continue along Pepper Street and turn left down Lower Bridge Steet signposted 'Handbridge'. Leave the city again via Bridgegate but do not cross the river. Turn right into Castle Drive where there is a car park on the left. From the car park walk back along Castle Drive to the Old Dee Bridge.*

ROUTE

1. *Cross over the Old Dee Bridge in the direction of Handbridge. Turn left down a short flight of steps and follow the path beside the river Dee. Continue, under the suspension bridge to a gate, which opens on to The Meadows. The riverside path curves around, through some willow trees and past a small ferry to the first of thirteen stiles. This stile marks the start of the water meadows, each bordered by a hedge with a stile. The stiles have deteriorated so that some are little more than well worn gaps in the hedge. However, stile ten is a concrete step ladder arrangement and fairly obvious. Proceed straight to stile ten where, shortly beyond the stile, a water pumping station appears on the right. Continue over two more stiles, past a disused quarry, to Heronbridge House with its beautiful garden, on the right. Look for a boundary stone marked 'CNR 1972' to the right of the next stile which confirms that you are at stile thirteen.*

2. *Cross the stile and turn right up the field beside Heronbridge House to an iron kissing gate opening on to Eaton Road. Turn right and walk up the road until you reach a stylish white house called 'Greenbank' on your right. Cross over the road and turn immediately left along a woodland path. Do not go through the metal gate facing Greenbank. The path backtracks before swinging right to join Dukes Drive, a splendid tree lined avenue. Turn right and continue to the end of the drive, marked by wrought iron gates. Pass through the gates to a roundabout. Turn right and cross Overleigh Road to take the next right which is Grosvenor Road. Continue up the road and over Grosvenor Bridge to the traffic lights. Turn left into Nuns Road and the start of the city walls.*

3. *Initially the wall passes alongside Nuns Road, over Watergate and then beside City Walls Road to a tower with a second tower offset to the left. At this point the wall turns right and continues with the canal on the left,*

45

the Chester Visitor's Centre. The walls are the best place to view the city. Outside the city walls there is much to see and in Summer the river is alive with people messing about in boats and the Groves are a pleasant venue from which to watch this activity. The Old Dee Bridge was once the only link with Wales but two new bridges including the suspension bridge give access over the river.

Refreshments The city centre has many fine eating places and the visitor will be spoilt for choice.

---

over two more gates to another tower where the wall turns right and passes the cathedral. Next is the beautiful Eastgate. Continue, over Newgate and bear right for the last time. The final section overlooks the Groves and River Dee. Turn right and leave the walls at Bridgegate. Pass under Bridgegate and return to the Old Dee Bridge from whence the walk started.

THE PARADE, PARKGATE

Parkgate and Gayton

Outline   Parkgate Parade ~ Gayton ~ Backwood Hall ~ Parkgate Parade.

Summary   The outward journey along the promenade and the lower edge of the golf course follows a comfortable, well defined path alongside the Dee estuary. There is a choice of two return routes. The lower one follows the course of the old West Kirby to Hooton railway line and is well surfaced and easy walking. The higher level route is more strenuous and goes around the top edge of Heswall golf course and through Backwood Farm before dropping down to meet the lower alternative route.

Attractions   Parkgate evolved, from a few dwellings clustered around the seaward gate of Neston Park, into an important port. Later it became a fashionable seaside resort, a fishery for shellfish and a centre for smuggling. These activities ceased as the river Dee silted up and the sea was replaced by permanent salt marsh, although each has left its mark on modern day Parkgate. Thus the promenade with its fishermen's and coastguard's cottages retains a strong seaside feel about it and local residents are working hard to conserve this historical gem in the extreme north west corner of Cheshire. As a visitor to Parkgate you are in good company for included in its list of famous visitors are John Wesley, Handel and Emma Lyon, later to become Lady Hamilton and mistress of Admiral Nelson. A clear day is essential if the fine view across the Dee estuary to the hills of North Wales are to be appreciated fully. There is nothing better than to sit on the old sea wall eating fresh shrimps and home-made ice cream, two local delicacies, and watch the antics of the seabirds foraging on the salt marsh.

Leaving Parkgate, the walk passes the old baths a popular meeting place in days gone by, currently converted into car parking and picnicing facilities for Wirral Country Park. The walk then continues around three sides of Heswall Golf Course to Backwood Hall. Both alternatives make use of the disused railway line which originally traversed the Wirral peninsula from Hooton to West Kirby. The top section of the walk strays into Merseyside. This charming walk has an air of timelessness, with much to recommend it.

Refreshments   Parkgate has a variety of teashops, ancient public houses and shops selling shrimps and home-made ice cream. The seaside

continued on page 50

47

Route 10

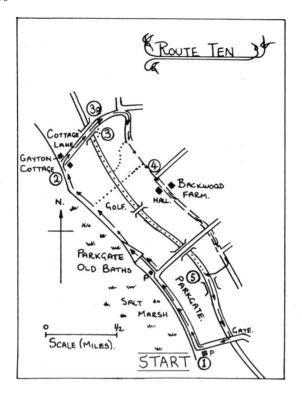

OYSTERCATCHER   black/white   43cm

Route 10

Parkgate and Gayton   5 miles

START   *The Old Quay public house (GR 289761) at the southern end of Parkgate Parade. Take the A540 from Chester along the Wirral Peninsula. Turn right, signposted 'Parkgate'. Follow this road down to The Parade, which is a promenade alongside the Dee estuary. Park on The Parade.*

ROUTE

1. *From The Old Quay walk along The Parade to a black and white building in the distance, which is The Boat House, another public house. Take the road beside the pub, signposted 'Gayton', along the side of the Dee to Wirral Country Park at Parkgate Old Baths. Follow the path between the salt marsh and the golf course to Gayton Cottage, which is where the houses restart.*

2. *Turn right up Cottage Lane, between Gayton Cottage and White Acre, to a bridge over the Wirral Way, where a choice of two routes exists.*

3. *The shorter route is found by crossing the bridge and turning immediately right down a track to meet the Wirral Way. Turn left, signed 'Neston', and follow the 'Way' across the golf course, under Backwood Hall Bridge, under Boat House Lane Bridge, to the wooden bridge at Brooklands Road. The two routes rejoin here. See instruction 5.*

3(a). *The main route continues up Cottage Lane to the crossroads at the top. Turn right into Gayton Farm Road signposted 'Parkgate'. This section of the route is way marked with a black footprint on a yellow circle. Bear right and then left down a stony lane, keeping Little Gayton Hall Farm on your right. Follow the way marked path along the top edge of Heswall Golf Course and across two fields to a kissing gate at Backwood Hall.*

4. *Take the farm road ahead, between Backwood Hall (right) and Backwood Farm (left) until it meets a road, Boat House Lane. Cross this road into Wood Lane, a rough stony road. Shortly after passing Brook Lane on your left take the waymarked footpath to the right, opposite Windy Knowe. The path drops down to a wooden bridge. Turn right, before the bridge, to join the Wirral Way. The two routes rejoin at this point.*

5. *Cross over Brooklands Road Bridge and follow the path through the*

atmosphere makes it an ideal place to start and finish this walk. There are no refreshment facilties on the remainder of the walk.

---

trees to Station Road. Turn right down Station Road and The Old Quay is at the bottom on the left.

DUCKS AT THE VISTRA MARINA

Wheelock to Alsager

Outline   Wheelock Wharf ~ Alsager ~ Hassall Green ~ Wheelock Wharf.

Summary   The walk includes two sections of disused railway line, the towpath of the Trent and Mersey Canal and field paths. The route is easy, level walking with the exception of a short, sharp inclined path from the fields up to the canal towpath for the homeward journey.

Attractions   A length of the former Audley colliery railway line provides a pleasant introduction to this walk. The old station with its picnic tables is an attractive feature, which together with the tree-lined path to the canal, is a sanctuary for wild flowers and small birds. The canal towpath runs alongside the Wheelock flight of paired locks, which are in constant use during the Summer months. The locks are visually and technically interesting and numerous stops will be necessary to watch boat movements through them. Children must be well supervised along this section because the locks are deep. Canal bridges and attractive terraced cottages, set against farmland and a golf course, add to the interest of this area. The tranquillity is suddenly interrupted by the roar of traffic as the M6 motorway passes overhead but this can be dispelled from one's mind by a visit to the Vistra Marina at Hassall Green. This charming spot, situated at lock 57, is worth visiting on both the outward and the return journey. The Post Office and General Store provide facilities for refreshment and souvenir shopping and the resident white ducks complete the tranquil scene. The next section follows the salt line through farmland before diverting through fields to the canal once more. There are large numbers of horses in the surrounding fields, many of them from the Alsager Equestrian Centre. The walk returns along the towpath of the Trent and Mersey Canal via Hassal Green to journey's end at Wheelock.

Sandbach is a little over one mile away and well worth a detour to see the famous Saxon Crosses, St Mary's Church and Ye Olde Blacke Beare, a part-timbered thatched building.

Refreshments   There are two public houses in Wheelock, the Cheshire Cheese and the Nag's Head Hotel. Sandbach has a variety of shops and eating places but by far the best venue for refreshment on a nice day is the Vistra Marina at Hassal Green or the nearby pub called the Romping Donkey.

Route 11

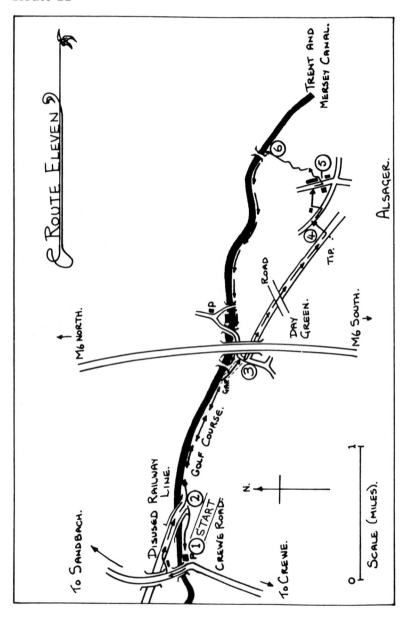

Route 11
Wheelock and Alsager   6 miles

START   *Wheelock Wharf (GR 751593). From Sandbach take the A534 in the direction of Crewe signed 'Wheelock'. After a mile look out for a public house called the Cheshire Cheese on the left. Wheelock Wharf is immediately before the pub.*

ROUTE

1. *From Wheelock Wharf walk to the Cheshire Cheese public house and turn right up Crewe Road (A534) until a bridge is reached. Do not cross the bridge but turn right along the footpath. Proceed past Station Houses and down to the disused railway line. Turn right, past the old station and continue to a bridge over the canal.*

2. *Turn left and follow the towpath for one mile. A gap appears in the fence on the right, fifty yards before canal bridge 148. This is the last canal bridge before the M6 crosses over the canal. Turn right through the gap, then immediately left to follow the track down to a road. Turn right and then left by the white house to join the Salt Line signed 'Rough Hollow'.*

3. *Pass under the M6 and follow the Salt Line until it meets a road. Cross the road and continue towards 'Alsager'. After some distance a tip appears on the right and a footpath cuts across the Sale Line at this point. This path is clearly marked by paired gates on either side of the salt line.*

4. *Turn left across a field to the road. Turn right and after eighty yards turn left into a lane indicated by a broken footpath sign. Take this lane and turn right at Bechton farm, across two fields to a road. Turn right and follow the road until the houses restart.*

5. *Immediately beside the drive of house number 6, almost opposite the Alsager Equestrian Centre, is a small gate. Turn left through this gate and follow the hedge around the house and then right, down to some trees. Turn left and then right over a stile, partially hidden in the hedge. Follow the field edge to the left until you come to a stile in the corner of the field. Continue straight ahead towards the houses. The path crosses a river and makes a short sharp ascent to rejoin the canal towpath at bridge 141.*

6. *Turn left under bridge 141 and follow the towpath all the way back to Wheelock Wharf.*

NOTE   *The new Wheelock Bypass will cross over the disused railway line and change the early section of this walk after the publication of this book.*

THE CHURCH OF ST. JAMES THE GREAT

Route 12   4–6 miles

Audlem

Outline   Audlem ~ Hankelow Mill ~ The Parkes ~ Mill Lane ~ Audlem.

Summary   This walk starts out from the bustling Audlem wharf and proceeds along the little-used towpath of the Shropshire Union Canal. It then follows a wide sweep through farmland and finally down a back lane into Audlem. The towpath is grassy and can be very wet after rain.

Attractions   Despite its small size Audlem is a perfect place for a family day out. Dominating the central square is the Parish Church Of Saint James The Great with the butter market below. The market was also the scene of bear-baiting. The wharf has been renovated and the Audlem Mill is now a pleasant canal shop and exhibition centre. There are two pubs, one at each end of the wharf, the well established Bridge Inn and the Shroppie Fly, which opened as a pub in 1970 and is a relative newcomer. It takes its name from fast passenger boats or fly boats which operated in the area. Audlem is famous for its flight of fifteen locks, which start above Coxbank and descend ninety three feet to finish at Moss Hall. Across the canal from Moss Hall is a beautifully preserved canal stable. From the lower lock the canal follows an embankment over the river Weaver, via an aqueduct, giving pleasant views of gently undulating farmland. Much of the land is used for milk production and large herds of Friesian cows are a common sight. Hankelow Mill has been tastefully restored for residential use. Sadly Audlem Old Mill, which gave its name to Mill Lane, has completely disappeared.

Re-entering Audlem from Mill Lane interesting architecture and attractive cottage gardens enliven the scenery. In conclusion, the towpath and the surrounding countryside are very unspoilt, with a rich and varied wildlife, worthy of preservation and respect.

Refreshments   Audlem is well provided for in terms of refreshment places. There is a fish and chip shop opposite the car park, a tea shop beside the Parish Church and home-made ice cream can be purchased from a shop nearby.

There are five public houses: The Bridge (canalside), The Lamb, The Lord Combermere, The Crown, and The Shroppie Fly (canalside). There are toilets in the car park at the start.

Route 12

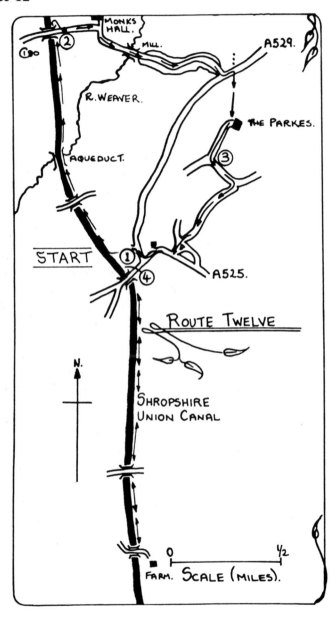

Route 12

Audlem   4–6 miles

START   *Audlem car park (GR 659437). Take the A529 from Nantwich, signposted 'Audlem' and follow this road into Audlem village. Soon after entering the village turn right into a clearly signed car park between the Police Station and Audlem Public Hall. Toilets are available in the car park.*

ROUTE

1. *Leave the car park and walk across the playing field to the canal wharf. At the wharf turn right, pass The Shroppie Fly and continue along the towpath to the second canal bridge, which is Bennett's Bridge, numbered 180. Pass under bridge 180 and turn immediately right up a narrow track beside the bridge to a small metal gate.*

2. *Pass through the gate and turn left up a farm lane, through two gates, to a 'T' junction at Monk's Hall Farm. Turn right and follow the lane around, over the River Weaver and past Hankelow Mill House on your left. Continue up the tarmac road until it meets the A529. Turn left along the verge and after fifty yards take the footpath turning right, on the other side of the road. This path is marked by a white kissing gate. Follow the hedge across the field, past a large house called The Parkes on the left and continue down the drive until it meets a road at The Parkes gate.*

3. *Turn left up a narrow road and then right, immediately past Mill House, on to an unmarked but clear footpath called Mill Lane. Follow this all the way down to a crossroads beside the bowling green. Proceed straight ahead to Stafford Street (A525). Turn right along Stafford Street and follow it around the Parish Church of Saint James. Turn right up Cheshire Street and the car park is on the left.*

4. *To extend the walk, return to the canal wharf and turn left up the towpath to investigate the other twelve locks which make up the Audlem flight. The locks are not numbered but the top lock is just past Coxbank bridge which is number 75. Return to the wharf by the same route.*

ELMER Route 7

Lymm

Outline   Agden Bridge ~ Lymm ~ Lymm Dam ~ Agden Bridge.

Summary   The initial walk along the canal towpath is easy level walking. The wide variety of paths around Lymm Dam, enable walkers to follow a gently undulating route to Church Green, avoiding any steep alternative pathways. The homeward journey follows paths and lanes around the back of houses and schools, before opening out into field paths for the final section to Agden Bridge. There are toilet facilities in Lymm and at Church Green.

Attractions   The canal towpath is interesting for boat enthusiasts because it passes several working marinas, where boats can be seen undergoing repairs in dry dock. It is a popular stretch for pleasure boating and always busy. Local canal bridges are named rather than numbered and Lloyd's Bridge was named after a family who lived and worked on the canals for two hundred years. Lymm village is a charming halfway rest stop and two features are well worth lingering over. One is the sandstone 'Cross' with its worn steps, three sundials and village stocks nearby. The other, found lower down in the village, is a pool known as Lower Dam, flanked on one side by the little white cottages of the Grove and on the other side by the Dingle. Do not dismiss this pool lightly for careful observers may see enormous fish swimming just below the surface. A pretty woodland path, called the 'Dingle' leads up to Lymm Dam. The Dam is a large expanse of water with many paths encircling it and a pleasant venue in which to relax and picnic before heading for home. Church Green is dominated by St. Mary's Church which with Lyam Dam as a backdrop creates a scene to make landscape painters and photographers go weak at the knees. The final section passes through the back lanes of Lymm and pleasant open farmland to rejoin Agden Bridge.

Refreshments   This is a good walk from the point of view of refreshment on route. Lymm has a variety of public houses including The Bull's Head, The Golden Fleece (canalside with a beer garden) and The Spread Eagle Hotel. There is a small tea shop at the bottom of The Cross. Reasonable shopping facilities exist in Lymm.

There is a public house at Church Green, called the Church Green. Ice cream vans operate from Lymm Dam at weekends.

Route 13

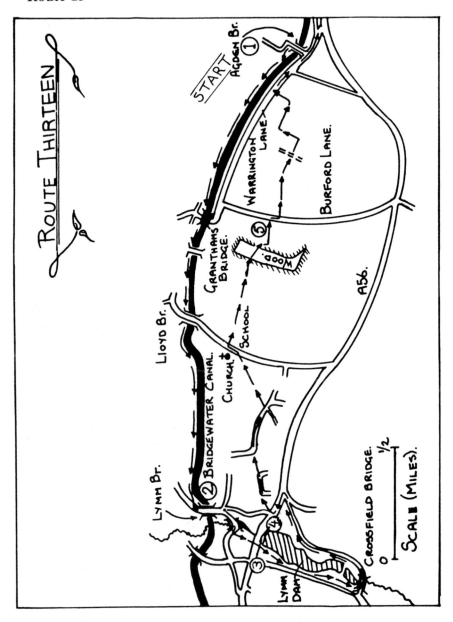

Route 13

Lymm
6 miles

START *Agden Bridge, off Warrington Lane, near Lymm (GR 716867). From Lymm take the A56 for a little over two miles towards Altrincham and turn left into 'Warrington Lane'. The turning is just past a bus layby and a small red postbox. Turn immediately right into a small side road where parking exists.*

ROUTE

1. *Agden Bridge, a small red brick bridge over the canal, can be seen across the field. It is reached by turning right down Warrington Lane and first right again. Cross over Agden Bridge and turn left on to the canal towpath. Continue along the towpath, keeping the canal on the left, to Lymm village. The route passes over Burford Lane, under Granthams Bridge, under Lloyd Bridge and leaves the towpath just before Lymm Bridge, by turning right at Reid House. The bridges are marked with their names.*

2. *Turn left and follow the road up and over the footbridge. Proceed down 'The Cross' to the bottom where the road bears right over a bridge. Cross this bridge and turn left up the secluded path called 'The Dingle' to the main A56. Cross over the main road and take the path ahead which encircles two stretches of water known as Lymm Dam.*
   NOTE *The walk around Lymm Dam can be omitted by turning left up the A56 to the Church Green public house and then continuing as for (4) below.*

3. *There are many paths around Lymm Dam. The simplest route is to take the wide path to the right of the Dam as far as the Avenue. At this point turn left over Crossfield Bridge and then left again signposted 'Crouchley Lane'. This leads to a car park at Crouchley Lane. Proceed through the car park and turn left along Crouchley Lane until it joins the A56. Turn left down the A56 ('Higher Lane') to the Church Green public house.*

4. *Turn right into Rectory Lane but do not go down this road. Take the unmarked footpath to the right of Rectory Lane, between two houses. This shortly becomes a road. Follow this road past a house called 'The Hatchings' to where the road bears sharp right. At this point turn left and immediately right along a path between a playing field and the back of some houses. Continue past a school and turn left opposite 'Grammar School Road'. Take the right of the two paths and head for the church in the distance. Turn left at the road and right at the church,*

on to a waymarked (yellow arrow) field path. Pass the cricket field and continue to a wood. Bear right through the wood to a field. Follow the waymarks along the field edge to Burford Lane.

5. *Turn right and then left, over a stile, beside the houses. This is the first of four waymarked stiles. Continue over the next three stiles to a rough cart track. Cross over this track and continue to the next hedge. Turn left and proceed to the next hedge. Turn right and then left leading to Warrington Lane. Turn right for the last time and the car is at the end of the lane on the left.*

THE SANDSTONE RIDGE

Route 14   4 miles

Bulkeley Hill and Raw Head

Outline   Bulkeley Hill ~ Rawhead ~ Bickerton ~ Copper Mines ~ Bulkeley Mill.

Summary   This is a physically demanding walk, climbing from the Cheshire Plain to the highest point on the Sandstone Trail at Raw Head (746 feet). The walk passes through mixed woodland and agricultural land specialising in dairy farming. Parts of the walk follow exposed sandstone edges and are unsuitable for children, unless carefully supervised. The well defined sandy paths drain quickly and are pleasant to walk on.

Attractions   The red sandstone ridge, which the walk follows, originated three million years ago when Cheshire was a desert. The red, iron based pigmentation of the sandstone makes an attractive contrast to the greens of the mixed woodland, covering much of the ridge. Sweet-chestnut trees are common and on a hot Summer's day the smell of pine trees gives the walk a Mediterranean feel about it. The triangulation point at Raw Head gives panoramic views stretching to Wales. Below the triangulation point is a large sandstone cave, one of many in the locality. Rumour claims that bandits used these caves as a base from which to rob unsuspecting passers-by.

Musket's Hole is an impressive natural amphitheatre. The walk used to pass through Tower Wood, but it has been re-routed along the outer edge of the wood so that the woodland could be developed into a pheasant shoot. The pheasant breeding pens can be seen as the walk drops down towards Chiflik, a name given to the area by a local Greek. The area just north of the A534 was mined for copper but a chimney is all that remains to mark the ancient pump house. The mining has been taken over by the local rabbit population, which is prolific and causing extensive damage to the sandstone around the mine.

Refreshments   The Bickerton Poacher is signposted from the walk. In addition to refreshments it offers the chance to enjoy a game of skittles in the old-style alley. There is a little shop in Bulkeley selling drinks and ices. At Higher Burwardsley the Candle Factory serves teas up to 4.00 p.m.

Route 14

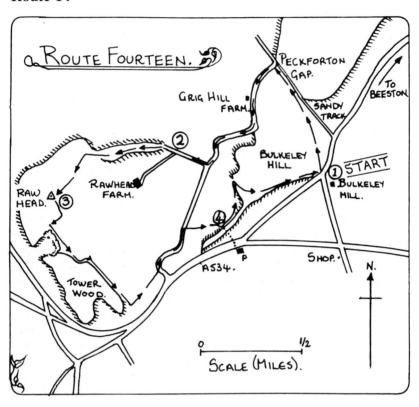

Route Fourteen.

PECKFORTON GAP.

TO BEESTON

GRIG HILL FARM.

SANDY TRACK

② BULKELEY HILL

RAW HEAD. △ ③

RAWHEAD FARM.

④

START ①
BULKELEY HILL.

A534.

SHOP.

N.

TOWER WOOD.

0   ½
SCALE (MILES).

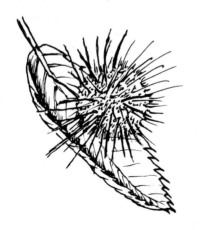

SWEET CHESTNUT

Route 14

Bulkeley Hill and Raw Head

START   *A very small layby near Bulkeley Mill (GR 529550). This is found by driving along the A534 (Wrexham Road) in the direction of Wrexham to a crossroads at Bulkeley. Turn right at the crossroads and park at the top of this road beside a sign saying 'Stone House Lane'. There are two more laybys on the main A534, before the crossroads, providing additional parking.*

ROUTE

1. *Pass through the gap in the fence and take the wide path to the right signposted 'Peckforton Gap'. Continue, past the inclined railway on the left. The route steepens and a wide sandy lane appears on the right of the path. Take either the footpath or the lane to the top, where a bridge shaped house leading into the Peckforton Estate (Private) can be found on the right. Turn left and follow the stoney lane, past Grig Hill Farm, to a point where a footpath can be seen signed to the right. This is a useful short cut but the main route bears left and then right before joining a small road. Turn right signposted 'Raw Head' and continue towards the farm as far as the drive.*

2. *Take the footpath straight ahead and after a short distance turn left into 'Conservation Woodland'. This section follows the Sandstone Trail, which is waymarked with a black footprint, overprinted with the letter 'S' in yellow. Stout fences also help to demark the path to, and beyond, Raw Head. Follow the well defined path to the trig point (OS BM S3124) at Raw Head.*

   NOTE   *There are some very high and exposed edges in the section of the walk leading up to, and immediately beyond, Raw Head.*

3. *Turn left at the trig point and then right down some steps. After a little way turn left and follow the waymarks, along the edge of Tower Wood. The walk drops down, and just past the pheasant rearing pens it leaves the Sandstone Trail by turning left on to a path, signed 'Copper Mines'. Turn left, signposted 'Poacher Inn' and follow the yellow arrows, past the copper mines on the right, to a small road. Turn left along the road. Turn right along a path signposted 'Bickerton Poacher'. Continue until a choice of routes exists. (To reach the Poacher, turn right down the dark path, shadowed by holly bushes. Climb over the heavy duty stile and walk down the field to the Inn.)*

4. *The main route continues straight ahead across the field between bracken. Bear left up the hill to a stepped stile. Cross the stile and turn right down the wide track, which returns to the start of the walk.*

DELAMERE FOREST

Delamere Forest

Outline   Linmere ~ Eddisbury ~ Barnsbridge Gates ~ Linmere.

Summary   There are many pathways in Delamere Forest but this walk focuses on two important forest routes, the Sandstone Trail and a cycleway, both clearly waymarked to provide easy passage through the forest. The sandy forest tracks drain quickly and the main routes are well metalled, creating good walking surfaces. The land is undulating with some steep sections. A circular easitrail, starting and finishing at Barnsbridge Gates, gives access to the forest for wheelchair users.

Attractions   Delamere Forest is a small remnant of the great forests of Mara and Mondrum that once covered much of Norman England. Large areas of the original oak woodland have been replaced by coniferous species, which thrive on the sandy, acidic soils. However, mixed deciduous trees still account for a fair proportion of the total tree cover. Delamere is a working forest, producing timber and tree seedlings for use through Britain. Specialist foresters monitor disease and use genetic manipulations to develop new varieties of trees, with improved resistance and hardiness. This living, working environment offers excellent recreational facilities and information on these and other aspects of forest life can be found in the Visitor's Centre. Management means that different areas of the forest are at different stages of maturity creating a range of natural habitats each with its own diverse fauna and flora. During the Summer months the large open clearings are covered in a mixture of bracken and foxgloves and later in the year fungi appear in abundance, under the trees. The forest attracts a rich variety of birdlife throughout the year and it is worth taking a pair of binoculars. The forest has wet land areas called mosses, which support the growth of specialised vegetation including sundews and sphagnum moss. The walk provides a unique but sadly rare experience to enjoy the dwindling Cheshire forests.

Refreshments   Having completed this walk Hatchmere is a pleasant spot to conclude the day's outing. Here a cafe and shop sell refreshments. There is an Italian Restaurant and two public houses, The Delamere Forest and the Carrier's Inn, overlooking Hatch Mere.

Route 15

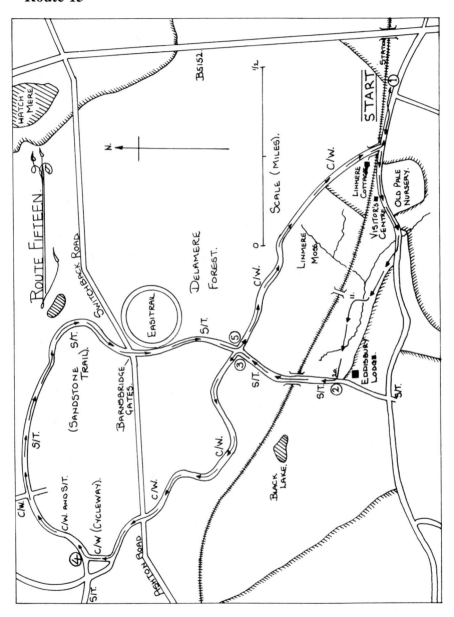

Route 15

Delamere Forest   5 miles

START   *The information board at Linmere (GR 553704). From Chester take the A51 and turn left at Tarvin on to the A54. Pass through Kelsall and turn left on to the A556. Turn left again, opposite the Vale Royal Abbey Arms, into Station Road (B5152). Continue along this road in the direction of Hatchmere and Frodsham to Delamere Station. Turn left into the lane signposted 'Linmere Picnic Area'. After a hundred yards turn right into the car park, where the information board can be seen on the left. There are toilets here.*

ROUTE

1. *From the information board turn left along the path, signed 'Forest Office & Forest Information', which passes through a small gate on to a road. Turn right and walk past the Visitor's Centre. Turn right, leaving the road via a path, signed 'Forest Trail'. After a quarter of a mile turn right, also signed 'Forest Trail' and continue to a post waymarked '11'. Turn left at the post, along a wide path and continue as it bears sharp left down a steep bank. The path crosses a small stream and continues straight ahead to a second post waymarked '20', where the walk joins the Sandstone Trail (S/T).*

2. *Follow the Sandstone Trail waymarks (a black footprint overprinted with the letter 'S' in yellow) for half a mile to a crossroads, created by a cycleway, cutting across the Sandstone Trail.*

3. *Turn left and follow the cycleway, across Ashton Road and continue to where the cycleway rejoins the Sandstone Trail. The cycleway is a rough stony track (shown as Road symbol on the map) clearly waymarked with a white bicycle.*

4. *Turn right and follow the Sandstone Trail to Barnsbridge Gates where car parking and toilet facilities exist. Proceed through the car park and take the 'Easitrail' just beyond the barrier. After a short ascent turn left and take the easitrail signed 'Visitor's Centre'. This follows the Sandstone Trail for a short distance before turning left. Continue to the crossroads and turn left, leaving the Sandstone Trail, to rejoin the cycleway.*

5. *Follow the cycleway to the railway bridge just beyond Linmere Cottages. Cross the railway bridge and turn left along the road for a short distance before turning left through the small gate to follow the woodland path back to the car park.*

WILLEYMOOR LOCK

Marbury cum Quoisley

Outline   Marbury ~ Willeymoor Lock ~ Wirswall ~ Marbury.

Summary   The early part of the walk is along the towpath of the Llangollen branch of the Shropshire Union Canal. The towpath is grassy and uneven but not difficult to walk on. In places the vegetation on either side of the path grows above head height giving the path a certain rustic charm. From Willeymoor Lock the route is straightforward but some of the footpaths approaching Wirswall are overgrown and not easy to negotiate. Beyond Wirswall the paths are easy to follow as they undulate over farmland.

Attractions   Marbury is a charming village in the south of Cheshire. Like many Cheshire villages it is overlooked by a prominent church and the view of St. Michael's Church across Big Mere, near the end of the walk makes a fitting conclusion to this route. Big Mere is one of two meres in Marbury, both of which are excellent bird-watching venues. A seat in the church grounds provides an ideal vantage point from which to watch the Canada Geese that breed on Big Mere. The Swan Inn, overlooking Little Mere, is the sole survivor out of five inns that once served Marbury. By day the village is a blissfully sleepy place but by night visitors pour into the Swan to enjoy the local hospitality. From Marbury the Shropshire Union Canal leads to Willeymoor Lock. The towpath provides a pleasant unspoilt walk through rural countryside. The journey continues through Wirswall and to Wicksted Old Hall, which is only a field's distance from the Cheshire–Shropshire boundary. At Wicksted, Gill Dale's Mushroom World makes an interesting diversion from the walk and her fungal creations will delight visitors, both young and old. The final stage of the walk passes through farmland, given over exclusively to dairy farming.

Refreshments   The Swan Inn in Marbury is an obvious choice for a drink and a meal, either before commencing the walk or at journey's end. The Willey Moor Lock is a public house on the canal towpath. It is the ideal spot to refresh flagging spirits at the halfway stage of the walk as well as to watch canal boats passing through the lock.

Route 16

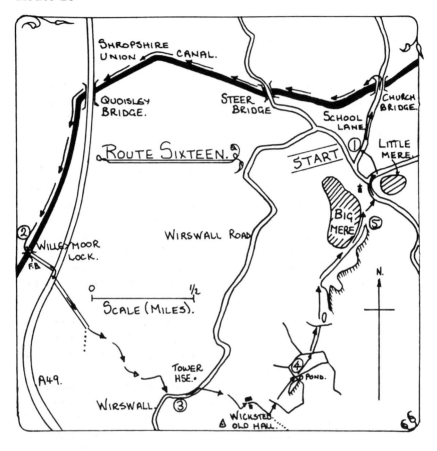

Route 16

Marbury cum Quoisley   6 miles

START   *Marbury Village Hall, School Lane, Marbury (GR 561459).*

ROUTE

1. *From the village hall, turn right down School Lane, as far as the Shropshire Union Canal. Cross over the canal via Church Bridge and turn left on to the towpath. Continue along the towpath, passing under Steer Bridge, then under Quoisley Bridge (number 25), past Quoisley Lock to the Willeymoor Lock, which is both a lock and a public house.*

2. *Turn left over the footbridge and walk up the lane to the A49. Turn right along the A49 and take the next left, signposted 'Bridleway'. Continue up this lane until it forks. Ignore the obvious track to the right, signposted 'Whitchurch'. Bear left along the footpath between two hedges. This is very overgrown at certain times of the year. Pass through the gate and continue straight up the sandy lane ahead. Turn left at the 'Bridleway' sign and after a short distance turn right and pass a house called 'The Spinney'. Continue to the road, which is part of Wirswall village.*

3. *Turn left and continue along this road until you come to a footpath on the right, signposted 'Gill Dales Mushroom World'. Follow this footpath, over the cattle grid and on to a second cattle grid at the entrance to Wicksted Old Hall (and Mushroom World). Turn left before the second cattle grid and proceed through the farmyard to a gate. Turn right through a second gate, adjacent to the first, and walk down the cart track. Halfway down the track a stile appears on the left waymarked 'SCW' indicaitng that the walk now follows the South Cheshire Way as far as Marbury. Turn left over this stile and cross the field to a second stile. Cross the stile and proceed across the field towards a clump of trees, passing to the left of the trees to another stile, waymarked 'SCW'.*

4. *From this stile bear left and walk diagonally down the field, in the direction of Marbury Church, which can be seen in the distance, once over the brow of the hill, to a stile. (Do not follow the obvious path down beside the hedge, at the right of this field.) On reaching the stile cross over and continue alongside the hedge, on your right, to a further stile. Cross this and, keeping to the left of the hummock, proceed straight to the wood ahead. Follow the woodland around to the left and continue with the wood on your right until Big Mere is reached.*

5. *Take the well defined track up the right hand side of the mere. Soon after the track opens out into grassland the official path turns right up the field to a gate. Pass through the gate and turn left up the road into Marbury. Turn right signposted 'Wrenbury', past the Swan Inn and take the footpath to the left, just before the telephone box. Continue up the field to a stile and then bear left across the playing field to a little path, behind the swings, leading to the Village Hall car park. The official path to the right of the school is not clear.*

LORD STREET,
BOLLINGTON Route 2

Appendices

LONG DISTANCE WALKS

For the more adventurous walkers a number of long distance paths exist in Cheshire, nine of which are indicated by letters on the introductory map:

A. *Wirral Way* .... *(12 miles)*
B. *Mersey Way* .... *(19 miles)*
C. *Weaver Way* .... *(20 miles)*
D. *Whitegate Way (Sandiway)* .... *(6 miles)*
E. *Sandstone Trail* .... *(32 miles)*
F. *Middlewood Way* .... *(11 miles)*
G. *Gritstone Trail* .... *(18 miles)*
H. *Mowcop Trail* .... *(9 miles)*
I. *Bollin Valley Way* .... *(60 miles)*

Cheshire Ring Towpath .... *Not shown*
South Cheshire Way .... *Not shown*
West Cheshire Waterways Ring .... *Not shown*

ROUTES IN ORDER OF DIFFICULTY

	Route	Mapsheet (1 : 25.00)
Whitegate Way and Newchurch Common — 3½–5 miles	8	SJ 66/76 and SJ 46/56
Middlewood Way & Macclesfield Canal — 2–6 miles	1	SJ 87/97 and SJ 88/98
Audlem — 4–6 miles	12	SJ 64/74
Marbury Country Park & Anderton — 3½ miles	7	SJ 67/77
Chester — Historic Walls & Water Meadows — 6 miles	9	SJ 46/56
Wheelock Wharf — Alsager — 6 miles	11	SJ 65/75
Parkgate — 5 miles	10	SJ 27/37
Lymm — 6 miles	13	SJ 68/78
Marbury cum Quoisley — 6 miles	16	SJ 44/54
Alderley Edge — 3 miles	3	SJ 87/97
Bollington to Rainow — 6 miles	2	SJ 87/97
Delamere Forest — 5 miles	15	SJ 47/57
Tegg's Nose — 3 miles	4	SJ 87/97
Mowcop — 6 miles	6	SJ 85/95
Rawhead — 4 miles	14	SJ 45/55
Macclesfield Forest — 5–6 miles	5	SJ 87/97

WET WEATHER ALTERNATIVES

Cheshire provides numerous and varied wet weather alternatives so that exploration of this fascinating county need not be confined to fine days. Two excellent sources of useful information for walkers are 'Enjoying Cheshire', a Cheshire County Council publication and 'Discovering the Cheshire Peaks and Plains', published by the

Cheshire Peaks and Plains Tourist Association. These, together with many Cheshire Countryside publications, are available from Tourist Information Centres, the telephone numbers of which are listed below:

Chester (Town Hall) 0244-340144
                                                                   0244-318356
Congleton (Town Hall) 0260-271095
Crewe .... 0270-583191 Ext 691
Knutsford 0565-2611
Macclesfield .... 0625-21955 Ext 115
Nantwich 0270-623914
Sandbach 093 67-60460

PUBLIC TRANSPORT IN CHESHIRE

A good network of public transport exists in Cheshire and a free guide to bus services called 'Out and About' is available from bus stations, libraries and the Tourist Information Centres listed above. Cheshire operates a number of information 'Hotlines' giving advice on the various bus services and special Sunday 'Adventurer Tickets'.

Bus 'Hotlines'
Chester 0244-602666
Crewe 0270-505350
Northwich 0606-815050
Wilmslow 0625-534850

Information on rail services is available from:
Chester 0244-40170
Crewe 0270-255245
Manchester 061 832-8353

CHESHIRE'S ARCHITECTURAL HERITAGE

Opening times vary and it is best to telephone for up to date information.

Adlington Hall (magpie architecture), near Macclesfield 0625-829206
Beeston Castle (13th century castle), near Tarporley 0829-260464
Bramhall Hall (magpie architecture).................................. 061 440 8400
Capesthorne Hall, near Chelford 0626-861221
Chester Cathedral.. 0244-24756
Gawsworth Hall (Tudor manor house)............................... 02603-456
Lyme Hall, Disley 0663-62023
Little Moreton Hall (magpie architecture), Congleton 0260-272018
Peover Hall (Tudor manor house), Lower Peover, near
    Knutsford 056581-2404
Tatton Park (Georgian house, deer park and farm), Knutsford 0565-54822

MUSEUMS

Boat Museum (canal boats and workshops), Ellesmere Port..... 051 355 1876
Cheshire Military Museum, Chester 0244-27617
Cheshire Heritage Centre (Chester history)......................... 0244-317948
Churche's Mansion (Elizabethan history), Nantwich.............. 0270-625933
Grosvenor Museum (Roman history), Chester...................... 0244-21616
Jodrell Bank (radio telescope and planetarium), Lower
    Withington 0477-71339
Macclesfield Museum (art collection and Egyptian history)....... 0625-24067
Macclesfield Silk Museum (silk heritage) 0625-613210
Mouldsworth Motor Museum (vintage cars and motoring
    history), near Frodsham 0928-31781
Nantwich Town Museum (local history) 0270-62710
Nether Alderley Mill (ancient working watermill), near
    Wilmslow 0625-523012
Paradise Mill (Victorian silk mill), Macclesfield.................... 0625-618228
Stretton Mill (working water mill), near Farndon.................. 0606-41331
Quarry Bank Mill (working cotton mill), Styal, near Wilmslow 0625-527468
Salt Museum (history of Cheshire salt), Northwich................. 0606-41331
Toy Museum (antique toys), Chester................................. 0244-316251
Warrington Museum (art, local history and archaeology)......... 0925-30550

OTHER ATTRACTIONS

Bridgemere Garden World (very large garden centre), near
    Nantwich 09365-239/381
Bridgemere Wildlife Park (bird and animal collection), near
    Nantwich 09365-223
Cheshire Workshops (candle making), Burwardsley............... 0829-70401
Chester Zoo.. 0244-380280
Stapeley Water Gardens, Stapeley, near Nantwich 0270-623868

SWIMMING AND LEISURE COMPLEXES
Cheshire provides many facilities for sport and these can be found in key centres including Chester, Congleton, Crewe, Ellesmere Port, Knutsford, Macclesfield, Nantwich, Northwich, Poynton, Runcorn, Warrington, Widnes, Wilmslow and Winsford.

Family Walks Series

All titles at £3.25.

Family Walks in the White Peak. Norman Taylor. ISBN 0 907758 09 6.
"The best Peak District short walks guide yet published." — *The Great Outdoors.*

Family Walks in the Dark Peak. Norman Taylor. ISBN 0 907758 16 9.
Companion to the first title.

Family Walks in the Cotswolds. Gordon Ottewell. ISBN 0 907758 15 0.

Family Walks around Bristol, Bath and the Mendips. Nigel Vile. ISBN 0 907758 19 3.

Family Walks in Hereford and Worcester. Gordon Ottewell. ISBN 0 907758 20 7.

Family Walks in the Downs and Vales of Wiltshire. Nigel Vile. ISBN 0 907758 21 5.

Family Walks in South Yorkshire. Norman Taylor. ISBN 0 907758 25 8.

Family Walks in the Wye Valley. Heather and Jon Hurley. ISBN 0 907758 26 6.

Family Walks in Mid-Wales. Laurence Main. ISBN 0 907758 27 4.

Family Walks in South Shropshire and the Welsh Borders. Marian Newton. ISBN
0 907758 30 4.

Family Walks in the Staffordshire Peak and Potteries. Les Lumsdon. ISBN 0 907758 34 7.

Family Walks in Cheshire. Chris Buckland. ISBN 0 907758 29 0.

Family Walks in South Gloucestershire. Gordon Ottewell. ISBN 0 907758 33 9.

Family Walks in Snowdonia. Laurence Main. ISBN 0 907758 32 0.

Ready Spring 1991

Family Walks in North West Kent.
Family Walks in Berkshire and North Hampshire.
Family Walks in the Teme Valley.
Family Walks in Sedgemoor, Avalon and Mendip.
Family Walks in Oxfordshire.

Other titles in preparation.

The Publishers, D. J. Mitchell and E. G. Power, welcome suggestions for further titles in
this series; and will be pleased to consider other manuscripts of regional interest from new
or established authors.